A New True Book

STAMPS

By Karen Jacobsen

This "true book" was prepared
under the direction of
Illa Podendorf,
formerly with the Laboratory School,
University of Chicago

CHILDRENS PRESS, CHICAGO

Pueblo pottery stamps

PHOTO CREDITS

Reinhard Brucker—2, 9 (right top and bottom), 16 (top row and bottom right), 20, 35, 36, 39, 41

Hillstrom Stock Photos: © Milt and Joan Mann— 4, 9 (left), 19; © W.S. Nawrocki—Cover, 13, 17, 24, 28 29, 31, 43

Scott Publishing Company—11, 14, 32, 33, 34, 44

A. Kerstitch—16 (bottom left), 26

James M. Mejuto—22

COVER—Current stamps of
          the United Nations

Childrens Press gratefully acknowledges Scott Publishing Company's assistance in coordinating the illustrative materials for this book.

Library of Congress Cataloging in Publication Data

Jacobsen, Karen.
  Stamps.

  (A New true book)
  Includes index.
  Summary: A brief beginner's guide to the quiet, but exciting hobby of stamp collecting.
   1.   Postage-stamps—Collectors and collecting— Juvenile literature. [1.   Postage stamps—Collectors and collecting]   I.   Title.
HE6215.J32   1983   769. 56′075   83-7591
ISBN 0-516-01709-8   AACR2

TABLE OF CONTENTS

A postcard from Andorra has two stamps because this tiny country in the Pyrenees Mountains is governed by both Spain and France.

4

STAMPS ARE IMPORTANT

It's fun to receive a
picture postcard in the
mail. On one side there is
a picture to look at. On
the other side, you will find
three things: your name
and address, a message,
and a postage stamp.

The name and address
are important because they
tell where to deliver the
postcard.

The message can be
important, too. It gives
some news and tells who
sent the postcard.

But what about the
postage stamp? Why is it
important?

The postage stamp is
proof that someone paid to
mail the postcard to you.
But there is much more to
notice about the stamp.

A close look shows a
picture of a man's head,
the letters "USA," then

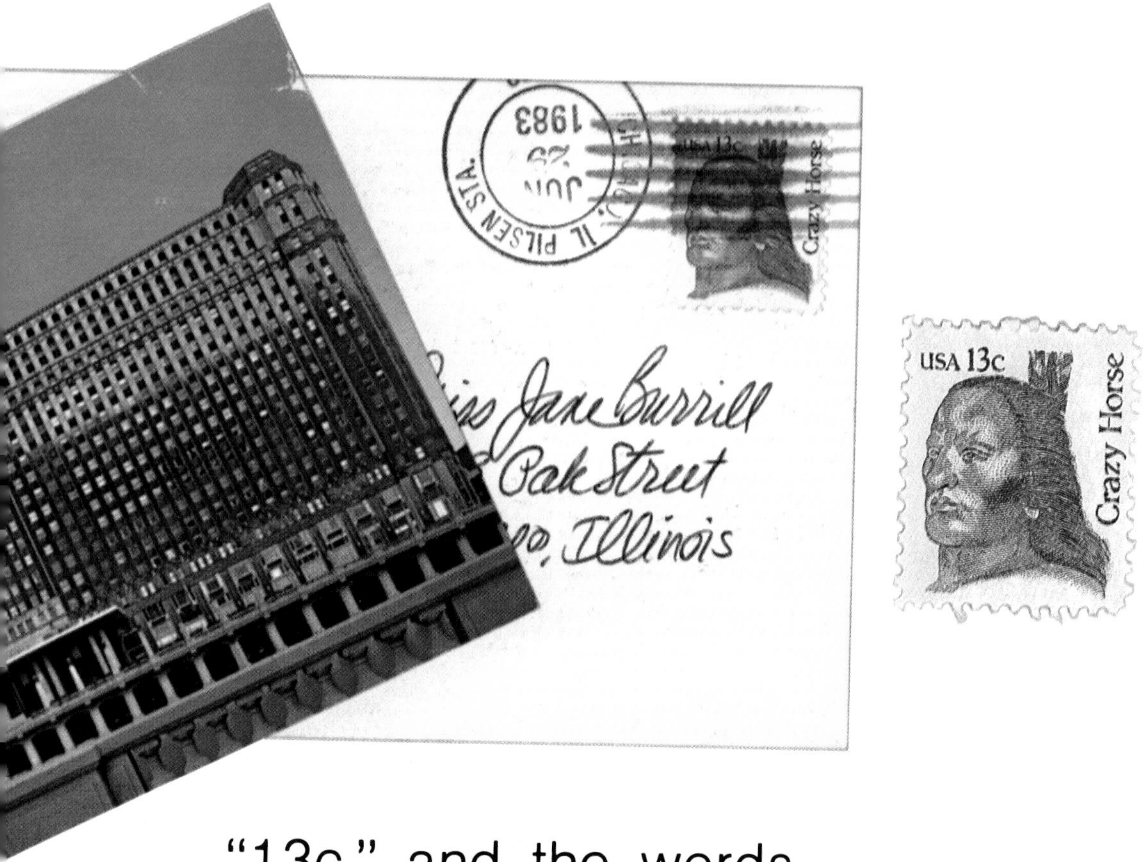

"13c," and the words "Crazy Horse." There is also some black printing over the stamp.

The picture is a drawing of Crazy Horse, a famous Native American leader.

The letters "USA" mean that the stamp is from the United States of America. And "13c" means that the stamp cost thirteen cents.

The black printing is called a cancellation mark. It is printed in the post office. It shows that the stamp has been used and cannot be used again.

Today more than one hundred countries print and sell their own postage

Left: Cancelling a stamp by hand
Above: A Russian stamp
Below: A Polish fish stamp

stamps. Each stamp shows
the name of its country
and a price.

Each country spells its
name in its own language.

9

STAMP DESIGNS AND COLORS

Two of the most interesting features of any stamp are its design and its color. Some stamps have simple designs in only one color. But most stamps are small, full-color pictures of people, places, or other subjects of all kinds.

Some countries use one stamp design for many years. But other countries

issue many new stamp
designs every year.

Sometimes new designs
are issued on the
anniversary of an important
event, to honor national
heroes, or to support worthy
causes and charities.

Many stamps are issued
simply because they are
pretty and people will like
to use them.

STAMP COLLECTING

The main reason for printing and selling postage stamps is to pay for the cost of delivering mail. Each stamp that is sold helps to pay for a country's mail service.

But there is another reason why postage stamps are important— people like to collect them.

Stamp collecting is one
of the most popular
hobbies in the world.
People of all ages and
from all walks of life
collect postage stamps.

A group of United States airmail stamps

Stamps from (left to right, top row) Paraguay, Redonda, Paraguay; (left to right, bottom row) Turkish Federated State of Kibris, France, Turks and Caicos Islands

For many people, collecting stamps is like hunting treasure. Each new stamp is a welcome addition to a collection.

Today there are more than 200,000 varieties of stamps. No one can own one of each kind. But it is interesting and rewarding to try to collect as many stamps as possible.

Some people collect only unused stamps. They must be like new and never used on mail. Mainly they collect single stamps. But they also collect pairs, strips, blocks, and panes of stamps.

Top row and bottom right: Blocks of United States stamps
Bottom left: A cancelled orchid stamp from Venezuela

Other people collect
used stamps. They look for
cancelled stamps in
excellent condition. Some
have special collections of
cancelled stamps on their
original envelopes.

Hawaiian
stamps from
the 1890s

OLD STAMPS

Whether used or unused,
old stamps are usually the
most valuable in a
collection.

The first postage stamp
was issued in 1840 in
Great Britain. It was
printed in black ink on

white paper. It showed a picture of Queen Victoria with the words "postage" and "one penny." Today, this stamp, called a "Penny Black," is very valuable because it is the oldest postage stamp.

In 1847 the United States government issued its first two postage stamps. The 5¢ stamp showed Benjamin Franklin and the 10¢ stamp showed George

A stamp museum

Washington. Today, either of these stamps in good condition can be worth thousands of dollars.

The value of any stamp depends on its condition.

Left to right: A stamp from Sierra Leone with an unusual shape, a United States Christmas stamp, a triangular stamp from Poland

The best grade for a stamp is "superb." Then comes "very fine," "fine," "very good," "good," and "average." The worst grade is "poor." Collectors keep stamps in poor condition only if the stamps are very rare.

STARTING A COLLECTION

Starting a stamp collection is easy. You can get lots of free used stamps. Just save every stamp on the mail that comes to your house. Ask friends and relatives to save stamps for you.

You can buy stamps, too. The postal services in many countries sell stamps and related materials to collectors. Stamps are also

for sale in stamp and
hobby shops.

Companies sell stamps
through the mail. Their
advertisements appear in

magazines. If you send them your name and address, they will send you a selection of stamps to buy or to return.

Many companies offer stamp mixtures for beginning collectors. A stamp mixture is made up of dozens of used stamps. You probably won't find any rare stamps in a stamp mixture. But you will find an interesting variety of stamps to start a collection.

An international stamp album

STAMP ALBUMS

The best place to keep stamps is in an album. A stamp album is a special kind of book with pictures of stamps on its pages.

There are many kinds of albums. Some have places for the stamps of only one country. But other albums have places for the stamps of many countries. They are called international albums.

The pages of international albums are usually arranged in alphabetical order, country by country. The stamp pictures on each page are arranged from the oldest

A book about stamps and a looseleaf notebook album

stamps to the newest.
There are blank spaces for
future stamps.

You can make your own
stamp album. Use a loose-
leaf notebook and lined
paper. Write the name of a
different country at the top
of each page. Add new
pages as you need them.

PREPARING AND SORTING

The next step is to prepare your stamps for display in the album.

First, remove any pieces of envelope paper that may be attached to the stamps. Just soak the stamps in clean water until they float free from the paper.

Current stamps of the United Nations

Try not to touch the stamps with your fingers. (There are natural oils on your fingers that can harm the stamps.) Use stamp tongs. They are specially designed to handle stamps safely.

An assortment of stamps from around the world

Use clean blotting paper to dry the stamps. Be sure to keep them perfectly flat as they dry.

Next, sort your stamps, country by country. You may find duplicates (more than one copy) of the same stamp. Pick the best copy to keep in your album. The best copy should have no folds or tears. Its perforations (the little notches all around the edge of the stamp) should be perfectly formed.

Keep duplicates together in marked envelopes. Trading duplicates with other collectors is a good way to get different stamps for a collection.

Duplicate stamps for trading are kept in a storage folder.

As you sort your stamps, you may find parts of a stamp set. A stamp set usually shows different pictures of the same subject. Most stamp sets

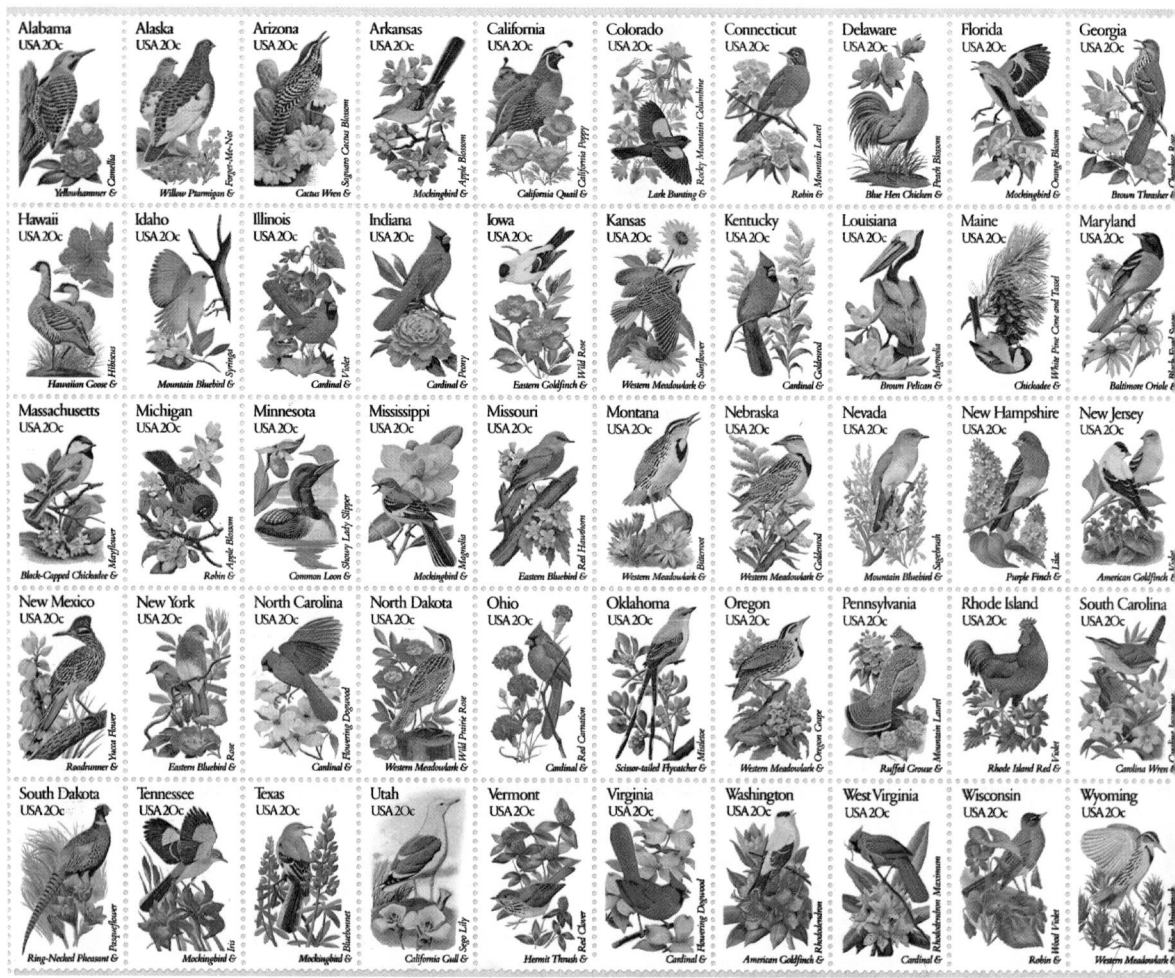

have the same print style.
This 1982 stamp set has
fifty different pieces. There
is a bird and flower design

for each of the fifty states. All of the stamps cost the same price.

Some stamp sets have a different picture and a different price for each stamp. In this 1894 set each portrait has the same frame and print design, but the stamps have different colors and prices.

PLACING IN ALBUMS

After your stamps are sorted, find places for them in your album.

It's easy to tell these stamps are from Paraguay. The name Paraguay is printed on each stamp.

These stamps say "Magyar." Is there a country by the name of "Magyar" in your album? Probably not.

Left: A diamond-shaped stamp from Hungary
Right: A circular stamp from Tonga

To find where this stamp belongs, turn the pages of your album, from country to country. Look at the words printed on the stamp pictures. You will find "Magyar" on the pages for Hungary.

"Magyar" means Hungary, so Magyar stamps belong in the Hungarian section of your album.

To fasten stamps in an album, use stamp hinges. They are small, strong paper rectangles. They have glue on one side.

To prepare a stamp hinge for use, place it glue side down. Then fold it up—at about one fourth of its length—to form a small flap.

Next, lightly moisten the glue on the flap. Then, stick the flap to the back of a stamp, near its top. Moisten the other flap and stick it on the stamp picture in your album. Press firmly with a clean piece of paper until the glue dries.

You may find some stamps don't match any of the pictures in your album. The stamps may be new

Stamps in a stock album

or the album may not have
a picture for every stamp
issued.

If you can't match a
stamp to a picture, fasten
the stamp in one of the
blank spaces.

STAMP CATALOGS

You can find out more about stamps in a stamp catalog. The catalog lists all of the world's stamps, shows pictures of many of them, and tells when they were issued. Some catalogs also give price information about stamps. Look for stamp catalogs in the library or in bookstores.

To find out even more about stamps and their

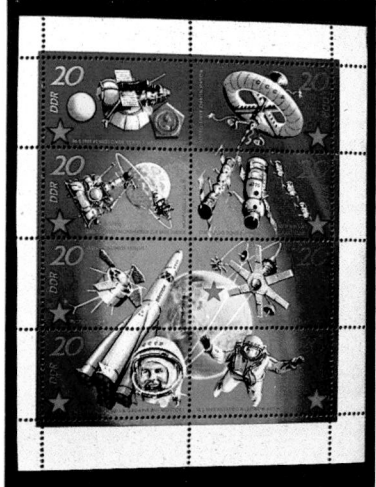

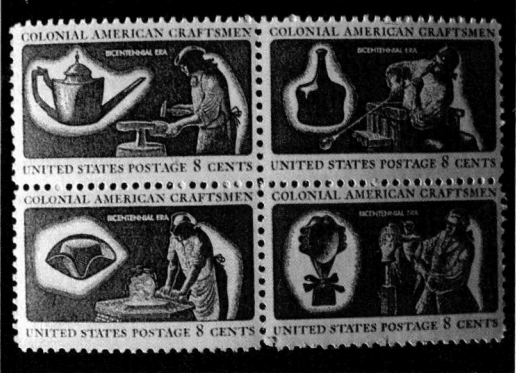

Top left: Spirit of St. Louis stamp
from the United States
Above: A block of stamps from
East Germany
Left: A block of American
craftsmen stamps

countries, use an atlas or
an encyclopedia. The more
you learn about stamps, the
more you will know about
geography, history, and foreign
languages.

SPECIAL COLLECTIONS

Many stamp collectors choose special subjects for their collections. They collect only those stamps that show pictures of their specialties.

Sports stamps are a favorite with many collectors. Almost every country in the world has issued some sport stamps.

Other favorite subjects are animals, flowers, and kinds of transportation.

An international collection of animal stamps

Either choose a special subject for your stamp collection, or try to collect as many different stamps as possible. It's your collection, so it's your choice.

Top row, left to right: Stamps from Cambodia,
Denmark, Italy, Argentina
Middle row, left to right: Stamps from Portugal,
Canada, Japan, Greece
Left: Stamps from Mexico and Brazil

A QUIET HOBBY

Stamp collecting takes
time—a little or a lot. It
also takes money—a little
or a lot.

As your collection grows, you see and own beautiful examples of art and design. You make discoveries and solve problems. Best of all, you find out many things about your own and other countries.

Stamp collecting is a quiet hobby, but it can be very exciting.

WORDS YOU SHOULD KNOW

General Glossary

anniversary(an • nih • VER • sa • ree) — a special date, observed
    yearly

charity(CHAIR • ih • tee) — an organization that offers help to those
    who need it

condition(kon • DISH • en) — state of being, shape

deliver(de • LIV • er) — to take something to another person or
    place

design(dih • ZINE) — pattern or decoration

foreign(FOR • in) — from another country

hobby(HOB • ee) — an activity for amusement and/or education

international(in • ter • NASH • ih • nal) — concerning two or more
    countries or nations

moisten(MOY • sen) — to dampen or wet lightly

notice(NO • tiss) — to observe

original(ah • RIJ • ih • nal) — first

portrait(POR • trit) — a picture of a person

proof(PROOF) — evidence to prove that something is true or real

receive(ree • SEEV) — to get something from another person

sort(SORT) — to separate into different groups

valuable(VAL • you • ah • bil) — having special worth

variety(va • RYE • ih • tee) — a display or different qualities

worthy(WUR • thee) — deserving honor or approval

Stamp Glossary

album(AL • bum) — special type of book for holding stamps;
    published albums have printed pictures of stamps and other
    information about stamps on their pages

block of stamps — four or more stamps connected in a
    rectangular shape

cancellation mark(can • sell • A • shun) — mark or lines printed over a stamp by the post office to prevent the reuse of the stamp

hinge(HINJ) — small, strong glascene rectangle with special glue on only one side; folded, moistened, and used to hold stamps in place

mixture(MIX • cher) — unsorted, mixed stamps sold in packages

pane of stamps(PAIN) — a sheet of many stamps connected together

perforations(per • for • A • shunz) — punched holes between stamps to allow easy separation

strip of stamps — three or more stamps connected horizontally or vertically

tongs(TAWNGZ) — special smooth-tipped tweezers made for safe handling of stamps

INDEX

About the Author

Karen Jacobsen has her own stamp collection. She is a graduate of the University of Connecticut and Syracuse University. She has been a teacher and is a writer. She likes to find out about interesting subjects and then write about them.